AF416181

RUMIS
BOOK
OF
COMFORT

Based on Quran, Authentic Hadeeth, and sayings of Truthful Scholars

Abu Ammaar

In the Name of God, The Most Merciful, The Bestower of Mercy.

The Almighty creates nothing
without a purpose.
God would not have created the
earth if
the galaxy did not need it.
If the earth did not need
mountains, God would not have
made them.
If there was no need for the sun,
the moon,
and the stars He would not have
created them.
He would not have created You
without a purpose.

∞∞

Do not be fooled, my believing
friend,
this world is not to be trusted.
It will intoxicate you with its
sweet poisonous drink.
It will make you forget your
responsibilities,
and then in the Hereafter,
you have to answer for your evil
deeds
in pursuit of this world.

To find your true purpose in life, you must start worshipping God. When you smile and be good to others it is the worship of God. When you pray five times a day it is worship. When you are good to your parents it is worship.

The worshippers of God love everyone and see everything in the world as good until someone does something that is pure evil.

∞∞

A truth seeker does not look beyond the apparent. What the senses perceive is the truth. Knowledge is there for everyone to learn.

Don't waste your life on non-existent hidden knowledge.

∞∞

When God wants to solve our
problems,
He will do it as and when He
wills.
Your task is only to be patient.

∞∞

God cannot be questioned.
It is you who will be questioned.

Enjoy the time with your friends.
Be good to your friends. Tell them
good things and warn them
against the bad. You should
frequently visit your friends. Take
a gift when you go. This will
increase the love. Love your
friend for the sake of God.

∞∞

You will only know a person when you talk to him. You will know whether he is a person who is concerned about this world or the Hereafter.

∞∞

God wants you to go to heaven, and therefore wants you to worship Him, and do righteous actions.

∞∞

God sends the trials of suffering
and pain
to cleanse you of your sins
so that you enter heaven sinless
and pure.

∞∞

Surrender and submit to God
if you seek the love of God.

∞∞

A carpenter does not cut a wood

out of cruelty

but to make something beautiful.

The trials you are facing today

have a wisdom that you will know

soon.

∞∞

Attend the funeral of your ego

and surrender to your Creator.

∞∞

Don't be self-absorbed

think about others as well.

∞∞

Don't swirl around like a mad

person,

worship God as the Prophet

(peace and blessings of Allah be

upon him) has taught you.

Any type of new worship not

taught by the beloved Messenger

of God (peace and blessings of

Allah be upon him) will not be accepted by God.

∞∞

Pilgrimage to Kaaba is a pillar of religion.

This ritual is a reminder of Prophet Abraham (peace be upon him).

Real spirituality is experienced with this pilgrimage.

∞∞

Having faith involves both hope
and fear.

You hope in God's Mercy while
fearing His punishment.

∞∞

After reading the words of God
in the Quran
you will not like to hear any other
words.

∞∞

I read a verse from the Quran and
my eyes
became longing and longing.
I heard a verse from the Quran
and
my ears were deaf to the world.

Read the Quran and you will see
The beauty and truth of God.

In this world of trials
you can not relax
even a moment,
otherwise, you will lose
your place in the Hereafter.

∞∞

This world is like a tree
and we as immature fruits cling to
it
not yet ready for Paradise.

∞∞

Open the window of your heart
and pray the night prayer.

∞∞

I am the slave of God and I
embrace the Truth. I abhor
everything where the
remembrance of God is not
present!

∞∞

There is no God but One God,
the One deserving our Worship.
Until we grasp this reality
we are lost.

∞∞

A dignified mind is one that can
hold faith; otherwise, what is the
use of the mind?

∞∞

When God offers you His
blessings, overflowing with
abundant milk, drink to your
delight!
And be grateful to God.

Don't shout.
Shouting weakens your argument.
Instead, calmly discuss.

You cannot do anything.
Only if God Wills you can.

∞∞

Not every prison is built of metal.
Position and status, reputation,
and wealth can also be prisons.

∞∞

Humans are ungrateful when they
cannot satisfy all their desires.
They forget all the things that God

blessed them with and that they
have already accomplished.

Islam is the Way brought by the
Messengers of God.
Jesus (peace be upon him) the
mighty Messenger of God came
with Islam.

After Jesus was raised alive there came Prophet Muhammad (peace and blessings of Allah be upon him). People who believed in Jesus must now believe in Muhammad (peace and blessings of Allah be upon him).

∞∞

Whoever professes to be a Muslim but does not act upon the way of the Messenger of Allah (peace and

blessings of Allah be upon him) is
not a Muslim.

Don't be alone. Stick with the
community of believers who
believe in the Messenger of Allah
(peace and blessings of Allah be
upon him).

The first three generations of
followers of the Prophet (peace
and blessings of Allah be upon
him) are on the truth.
Do what they did.
Take your religion from them.

∞∞

The community of believers is on
the truth even if they are a
minority. They follow the
Messenger of God (peace be upon
him). They don't follow their

desires. They don't innovate new
things in the religion.

∞∞

Anything new introduced in the
religion will be rejected.

∞∞

Our religion has been made
perfect by God.

∞∞

Don't negate the Names and Attributes of God. The Quran is the Word of God, His inspiration, and revelation. It is not created.

∞∞

God speaks. The god which does not speak is not god.

∞∞

Idols don't speak.

∞∞

Ask God for anything and He will respond to your invocation.

∞∞

We have the Quran and the way of the Prophet (peace and blessings of Allah be upon him) now. There is no excuse for misguidance.

∞∞

Don't take the devils as your protectors and helpers instead of God.

∞∞

The truth is clear in the Book of God, the way of the Messenger of Allah (peace and blessings of Allah be upon him).

∞∞

Religion came from God. It was not founded by the intellect or views of men. Its knowledge is with Allah and His Messenger (peace and blessings of Allah be upon him).

∞∞

The Companions of the Messenger of Allah (peace and blessings of Allah be upon him) are on the truth. Whoever opposes the Companions in any of the matters of religion has certainly disbelieved.

∞∞

He who does an action that is not in conformity with the Quran and the *Sunnah* [which is the way of the Messenger of Allah (peace and blessings of Allah be upon him)] then his action will be rejected.

∞∞

Make your Religion for Allah alone. Free yourself from associating partners with Allah. This is known as *Shirk* (polytheism).

∞∞

Don't be a slave to your desires.

∞∞

Being cautious of your desires will
save you from destructive sins
such as worshipping idols, stones,
trees, and graves.

∞∞

None of you truly believes until
his desires follow what the
Messenger of Allah (peace and
blessings of Allah) came with.

∞∞

The Messenger of Allah (peace and blessings of Allah be upon him) did not leave anything except that he explained it to his followers.

∞∞

The beard and Hijab are not in the heart.
Faith is shown in actions.

∞∞

Fill your ears and eyes with the Quran and remembrance of Allah. Build your faith.

∞∞

We will never go astray if we adhere to the Book of Allah and the Sunnah.

∞∞

The best of the people are those of the Prophet's (peace and blessings of Allah be upon him) generation, then those who came after them, and then those who came after them.

∞∞

If you obey most of those on this earth, they will mislead you far away from Allah's path.

∞∞

Beware of forbidden matters.

∞∞

People never introduce something new in the religion except that they lose the like of it from the Sunnah.

∞∞

Fear Allah, and listen and obey your leaders.

∞∞

You should not be silent when you see a wrong. You should not be silent regarding the one who has deviated from the truth.

∞∞

Don't dispute and debate. They generate doubt in the heart even if you are successful in the debate.

∞∞

We should accept the Quran and
Sunnah as they have come. The
Lord should not be talked about
except as He has described
Himself in the Quran.

∞∞

Allah knows what happens to His
creatures in this world and what
will happen to them in the
Hereafter.

∞∞

The Most Merciful, that is Allah,
rose over the Mighty Throne
in a manner that suits His
Majesty.

∞∞

There is nothing like Allah.

∞∞

Nothing is hidden from Allah, in
the earth, or the heavens.

∞∞

Those whom you call upon besides Allah cannot even create a fly.

∞∞

Allah's knowledge encompasses every place and no place is hidden from His knowledge.

∞∞

It is Allah who makes you sleep
and then wakes you up.

∞∞

The believers will see Allah with
their own eyes on the Day of
Resurrection.

∞∞

The good and evil actions of the
slaves of Allah will be weighed on

the Scale on the Day of
Resurrection.

∞∞

The dead are either punished in
the grave or given bliss till he or
she is resurrected on the Day of
Resurrection.

∞∞

The Prophet (peace and blessings of Allah be upon him) will have a pool on the Day of Judgement.

∞∞

The Prophet (peace and blessings of Allah be upon him) will intercede on the Day of Resurrection for the sinful Muslims.

∞∞

Paradise and Hell will never cease to exist and will remain forever.

∞∞

Knowledge of Allah should not be limited. The knowledge of the creature is certainly limited.

∞∞

There is no compulsion in religion.

∞∞

Everything that Allah has
ordained to perish will perish.

∞∞

Be content and patient with the
Decree of Allah.

∞∞

Whatever has afflicted you would
not have missed you.

Whatever has missed you would
not have afflicted you.

∞∞

There is no creator along with
Allah.

∞∞

When you fall ill, Allah rewards
you for your illness.

∞∞

Allah admits believers into Paradise out of His Mercy based on their actions.

∞∞

And your Lord is not at all unjust to His slaves.

∞∞

Do not oppress one another.

∞∞

The Companion had the best and most perfect of the hearts.

∞∞

Obey Allah and obey the Messenger (peace and blessings of Allah be upon him).

∞∞

Indeed in the Messenger of Allah, you have a good example to follow.

∞∞

It is obligatory to act upon the sayings of the Messenger (peace and blessings of Allah be upon him).

∞∞

Pray like the Prophet (peace and blessings of Allah be upon him).

∞∞

None of you truly believes until he loves for his brother what he loves for himself.

∞∞

The one who sees an evil should change it with his hands.

∞∞

Dislike the sins and its people.

This is a part of faith.

∞∞

Repentance is an obligation on the servants.

∞∞

Allah does not forgive that partners should be set up with Him. He forgives everything else to whom He wills.

∞∞

The Sunnah is Islam and Islam is Sunnah.

∞∞

Islam began as something strange. It will return to being something strange.
So, give glad tidings of place in Paradise to the strangers.

∞∞

That day money will be of no benefit,
neither offspring,
except one who comes to Allah with a sound heart.

∞∞

O you who believe! Fear Allah as
He should be feared and die not
except in a state of submission.

∞∞

O you who have believed, fear
Allah and say just words. Allah
will then amend for you your
deeds and forgive you your sins.
And whoever obeys Allah and His

Messenger has certainly attained
a great victory.

∞∞

There is a morsel of flesh in the
body which, if it be whole, the
entire body is whole, and if it is
diseased all of it would be
diseased, truly it is the heart!

∞∞

Never has anyone avenged except
that it brought humiliation down
upon himself;
so, when he forgives and pardons,
Allah raises him in glory.

∞∞

When a person recites the Qur'an
and thinks about what it means,
this is from the most powerful
way to hold him back from sins.

∞∞

Indeed, the knowledge is religion, so, look to see from whom you take your religion.

∞∞

Do not accept praise you do not deserve. If you do accept such undeserving praise then you may be hit by criticism you do not deserve.

∞∞

Have good thoughts of your Lord. He forgives those who repent, responds to those who call upon Him, and gives those in need of what they need.

∞∞

Seek Allah's help, pray the *Istikharah* prayer asking Him to grant you what's best in a decision, and then be optimistic.

∞∞

Show a little compassion and be a little easy to deal with when you give advice.
Give it in a nice way that creates conviction and leads to acceptance.

∞∞

Don't let your hatred for a person stop you from being just with him.

∞∞

Tell people good things that will make them feel happy.

∞∞

Make Allah the most important of your priorities.

If you do this then everything else will be put in order with His permission.

∞∞

Anyone who would love to have
Allah open his heart for him,
or to enlighten it,
then it is up to him to refrain
from talking about matters that
have no meaning to him;
to forgive sins and keep
themselves free from acts of
disobedience;
and to do righteous actions in
secret.

So, if he were to do so, Allah
would enlighten him with
knowledge.

Everyone should have times when they sit alone, remember their sins and then seek Allah's forgiveness for them.

∞∞

Everyone will be happy and sad, but you should turn your happiness into gratitude to Allah and your sadness into patience (sabr).

∞∞

Sit with the elders, mingle with the wise, and enquire from the scholars.

Wear what you want and eat what you want, as long as you avoid two things: extravagance and arrogance.